the Devastation
Jill Alexander Essbaum

Cooper Dillon Books
San Diego, California
www.CooperDillon.com

Cover Art & Design: Max Xiantu

ISBN: 978-0-9841928-1-6

Acknowledgements:

The author wishes to thank Eric Bourland and Jessica Piazza
for their help with the initial draft of this poem, and the edi-
tors of Cooper Dillon, Adam Deutsch and Colleen Ryor, for
deciding to publish it.

The
Devastation

Jill Alexander Essbaum

Cooper
Dillon

For Michelle and Paige.

There is no-thing I want.

No.

There are a thousand things I want.
Each begins with going back in time.

(This is a prayer.)

Years younger, it is a different cross I'm nailed to.

All my charms, all my conniving.

My doings and my don'ts.

Impossible paths. Impassable boths.

(I will. I won't. I will. I won't.)

Years ago, I was old in my adulteries.

From deep beneath the snow somebody tempted me.

From underneath snow-sodden sidewalks,

      fissures and chinks slotted open.

I was beaten like a woman.

I was eaten like a woman.

I was smitten with paramours and paracletes.

Ever nearer to thee, but never near enough.

(Bluntly: Heaven's a bluff.)

For what cannot be trusted can't be seen.

And obsession is a cure for no-thing.

Like:

Coming back from Hell to take shelter in another

Hell.

Like:

Seeking the arms of death as if they were

       my mother's arms.

Like:

The savor of a first or final kiss.

                         (Like: *This.*)

But this story—*mine*—is as ordinary as chalk.

Prelusion: Years of extravagant agony.

Postlude: Dead as dead is, or can be.

The Mean, Medial, Middle:

Everything else.

A single, wagging finger.

A syphilitic beggar.

What milk. What honey.

(Whatever.)

From a roof in this weather, a woman like me might
    jump.

                            (I haven't.)

But scruple and doubt are my meat and my bread.
All that I behold is death.

                            (Never-the-less.)

So the first shall be lost.
And the thirst shall be lasting.
I fast but to speed on the end.

Not if but when.

                   (Is there no benediction for the skin?)

I have sawed through my sorrows

Like a jeweler would facet quartz.

But the eye is on the sparrow, not the whore.

Wait. There's more.

I am the carcass that circles the vulture.

I am the snakebite your venom depends on.

My heavy heart's your matter of opinion.

I am your pinion. The merest of gears thereamong.

(Is there no benediction for the tongue?)

And I wear your spikenard crown of spiky thorns.
Very well then, I should say, and then make sure
      of certain sad, last thoughts.
Where did I go wrong?
When can I go home?

                               (Why am I alone?)

How many knocks on the door have I fallen
        in love with?
The Gunsmith's wretched pounding.
The Cooper's timorous rapping.
The Saddler's addling whacks.

It is a past that's never over.
A past not even *past*.

So I cache myself in a castle on a hill.

I hoard quill pens and quilts.

(And pills.)

So I fill my hands with the shards of infinite ardors.

A generous cargo of *ohs* and *oh wells.*

And a strange half-wish to be a ghost.

It is the thing I wish for *most.*

But talking to the dead is the least of my crimes.

(When, then. Like the car they were riding in...)

I've been my sins. I'll be them again.
Christ, the bottle's empty. Turn this water into gin.
Here be the marrow. There be the bone.
Tomorrow, a gun.

And so it begins.

I wend through aeons of your gutters, Father.

Your eyes so black, so blatant, so bothered.

Your angels, too fragile.

Your answers, too manifold.

Your porridge, too cold.

What untold anguish.

You refuse to explicate.

My own regret, too late to face.

And my own face too plain to pray for.

Years ago, I gave over to my own heart's lust.

Love, like a muscle, leapt up, leapt up.

Today, all my dear ones are dust.

Oh praise. Oh prize.

As *woods* are to *wise*.

As *woulds* are to *whys*.

As *woulds* are to *wounds*.

Never rely on desire to tell you the truth.

I told the truth on a regular basis.

I was the saddest I knew.

You were the sadist I knew.

And the distance between the two.

And the mist that lifted off the moat.

(Is there no benediction for the throat?)

I know little of interims, blister pearls, or boats.

But the lamb is in the cabin.
And the jasper is in your grasp.
And the asp is on my breast.

I confess:

MAY I BE TORMENTED WHEREVER I AM.

In my jittery, haunted insomnia.

In my eighth and thirtieth year.

In the crisis my sky derives from.

In the terrible lurch that my heart gives.

In the sieve that is your heart where I have sifted

      swiftly through.

In the cruel, contorted corner of this merciless room.

In the I of your storm.

In farm fields and caves.

In the grave.

In gray, gaping enclaves.

In a trophy case, my name engraved upon *Last Place.*

In every bitter broth I sup.

In the abstract eye of the paradise moth.

In the bleak, oblique beatitudes recited

      to the sisters of your harem.

In the innuendos I befriend.

In the end which comes no matter how I beg

      forestalling it.

Or in the curse word I refrain from calling it.

In slim tremors of bliss.

(In: *This.*)

In the lifetimes I will live in simple instants.
In every dissimilar *for instance*.
In the whisky I toss back in a single salute.
In the fullness of all my futility.
In my frailty.
In the slope of even the loveliest shoulders
        which can bear but *so much*.
Tell me, tell me, tell me who you love.

(.)

There is no logic to the Word.

I am a blotch on your collar. A blemish on your record.

I float in your shallows like tears atop water.

Devil's daughter.

Everything has an over.

(Is there no benediction for the lover?)

Your weak priests scream to abbreviated moons.

I'm criminal in my deceptions.

My pretensions are lachrymal, acrimonious, alchymical.

There is no benediction for the accidental.

Oh Beast, I put thy mark upon me.

(Have mercy! Look gently!)

Oh Beast, I betrothe my woe to the rosette guilloche
     of your palace.
Oh Beast, I proffer my soul to the mould
     into which you have poured me.

(Poor me.)

Yes I will kiss your gristmill.

And I will spill the gristle.

And I will wrestle your messenger.

And I will dive from the very trestle.

That will be the last of all I ever do.

Except cry out for you.

Jill Alexander Essbaum's publications include the full-length collections *Heaven*, *Harlot*, and *Necropolis*, and a chapbook of sonnets, *Oh Forbidden*. She is a 2013 NEA Fellow in Poetry, an associate editor for the online journal *Anti-*, and a blogger for the *Best American Poetry* blog. She's presently at work on a novel vaguely based on the time she spent living in Zürich, Switzerland. She believes most firmly that wit trumps irony, clever beats disaffected, and, in all things, sincerity is key. Find her at JillAlexanderEssbaum.com

Cooper
Dillon

www.ingramcontent.com/pod-product-compliance
Lightning Source LLC
Chambersburg PA
CBHW050429110726
47899CB00008B/2915